White River Blues

COLLECTED POEMS OF JANE ULYSSES GRELL

Dedication

To the memory of my dear friend, Liz Mann,
who held my hand through many a bend in the river.

Papillote Press
London and Roseau, Dominica

Acknowledgements

My thanks to Lerlin Woodrow, for invaluable help with word processing.

Thanks also to student-tutors Simon Attang, Ethan Grant and Aagin Roy of Holy
Family College in collaboration with Waltham Forest, Antigua&Barbuda and
Dominica Twinning Association, as part of a successful and on-going Silver
Surfers Project.

First published in Great Britain in 2016
Papillote Press
23 Rozel Road
London SW4 0EY
www.papillotepress.co.uk

A CIP catalogue reference for this book is available from the British Library

ISBN: 978 0 9931086 4 8

Book and cover design: Andy Dark
Typeset in Constantina

Printed by Imprint Digital, Exeter, UK

White River Blues has been produced by the Papillote People's Press,
a book production company under the Papillote Press imprint

Papillote Press
London and Roseau, Dominica

Contents

Introduction

The title *White River Blues* comes from the name of the river in the village of Delices, where I was born, on the small Caribbean island of Dominica. The White River was the hub of the community. Of a slight opaqueness, due to sulphur emissions from the Boiling Lake, high up in the mountains, the White River has always seemed a fascinating silent witness. People came from surrounding hamlets to fish, wash and bathe while their washing dried on large, hot, sun-baked stones. Women arrived for their obligatory dip in the estuary, nine days after childbirth; this was a sort of ritual cleansing, granting permission to resume normal life. Born-again Christians and Jehovah's Witnesses regularly came for baptism by immersion. Daring youth would pit their strength against the gigantic waves of the Atlantic, sometimes ending in fatalities. The river also had to be crossed on foot when villagers travelled to the town of Roseau for the sale of their produce and the weekly shopping. Inevitably, someone slipped and fell, as did the frail elder who contracted pneumonia and died as a consequence. Indeed my grandfather, Anda George, was swept away one stormy day on his way home from his garden near the Victoria Falls; his body was never found. More recently has come a different sort of tragedy. In the wake of Tropical Storm Erika, which devastated Dominica on 27 August 2015, the once vibrant White River estuary has been reduced to a shapeless sandy bed of boulders and small pools, while the lives of hundreds of Dominicans have been brutally disrupted.

The poems in this collection were written over a period of almost three decades - from the mid-1980s to 2015. The latest ones were inspired by Erika, the force of which I actually experienced while on holiday at the time. Most of them are based on experiences of living and working in London and Dominica. They touch on snippets of life in their varying phases both joyful and sombre, where hardships are met with the fighting spirit of survival portrayed in the Blues songs of the African-American people.

Jane Grell

Other works by the same author

For children:
Dr Knickerbocker and Other Poems
A New Life in Britain

Poetry:
Praise Songs

Also published in the following anthologies:
Voices Memory Ashes – Lest We Forget: an anthology of Caribbean
Women Writers
IC3: The Penguin Book of New Black Writing in Britain.
Dominica, a Small Caribbean Island

Erika

unforgettable
death, damage and destruction
call her Erika

Where Ignorance is Bliss...

Tropical Storm Erika followed hot on Danny's heels.
Quietly, so unobtrusively she came;
no wind, just a gentle breeze
that stirred through the leafy trees.
Shafts of lightning, a few peals of thunder

but it was the rain, twelve hours of downpour

as without let, the mist-laden sky kept up her weeping.
From the kitchen doorway when it finally subsided,
we watched as busy rivulets rushed down drains
as mini waterfalls sprung out of every crevice of an adjacent wall.
We shook our heads the next day on hearing
the news bulletin advising workers to stay at home.
A public holiday on account of a little rain?
We scoffed in our ignorance.
Without access to radio, TV or Internet news
how could we have known of villages submerged
of schools and churches destroyed
of crops and livestock obliterated
of bodies and bridges washed away
of land-locked folk who needed helicopters to fly in basic aid?
Our belated wisdom, now mocking us,
seemed far, far worse than folly
as our sadness and survivors' guilt set in.

Storm Erika, Spirit-god or Impostor?

Stealthily she tiptoes over Dominica, a Moko Jumbie on stilts
and for an uncannily long time holds her breath.
With naked malice she finally exhales
upon the shrivelled upturned faces of the rain-gods
who had slumbered through the rainy season.
Chiding themselves for their shameful negligence,
they shed copious tears of contrition
from which the rivers, who had thirsted throughout those arid months,
now drank and drank till their swollen bellies burst.
Slowly at first they sipped, gulped then guzzled to excess
and, goaded to a red-hot lust for vengeance
they rushed and rampaged, cascaded and stampeded,
breaking their banks, scorning boundaries, tearing down walls.
They ripped fences, uprooted trees, kicked in roads and bridges
and swept them out to sea, dragging along
houses and humans alike.
Turning car parks into murky swimming pools
they lifted and smashed up ten ton vehicles
as if they were no more than plastic toys,
finally subsiding after twelve hours of mayhem.
Erika, sinister voyeuse, gleefully approves it all
and ruffling the treetops, she leads them in a funereal parting dance.
Mission accomplished, she tightens her steely cloak about her
and as silently as she'd arrived, slips surreptitiously away.

Displaced

Nurse, I need some light to drive away the shadows
swallowing up the walls of this strange place
Nobody warn me river would come and take away my house
my garden and my fowls
Yesterday, I see such strange things too
a big tree walking tall down a mountainside
I see it with my own two eyes, I tell you
and when it reach our village
it open its mouth wide, wide and start to laugh
That tree was pure evil
I try to hide, but where?
In the mud, under a rock or the skirts of a current?
It nearly drive my dogs mad, poor things
They send helicopter to bring us here, me and my neighbours
But I see only strangers, no one I know
and nothing but bedbugs and cockroaches crawling about
If I was back in my little house, the chickens woulda gobble them up
    so fast
but as you know, all my chickens gone, roaming the streets or dead
And as for me, I here in shadow-land with cockroaches for company
doing the dance of death upon my grave even before I close my eyes
    aie, aie, aie
Nurse, for pity's sake, do something before I lose my mind.
Make them go away and bite somebody else, non.
And Nurse, please, please, when can I go home?

Grand Inquisitor

Last night, the grand inquisitor paid us an unexpected visit
and with the water-logged tip of his fiery sword
fatally marked the brow of random victims
a carpenter, his chisel suspended in mid air
an expert bush-tea maker and soother of childbirth pains
a baker of mouldy breads
a teacher, ever railing against superstition
a pair of brothers distilling the aromatic oil of bay leaves
a toddler in its mother's arms
a righteous preacher with entertaining rants
a grandfather in his dotage
a minder for half the village children
three deep-sea fishermen
a teetotal rum-shop keeper
two drunken wood-cutters and builders
and an arrowroot huckster in her prime

Today, in our cramped little cemetery
above an ocean-kissed ridge
eighteen freshly dug graves lie side by side

In the dark, we lie awake for hours
listening to the doleful murmurings of wind, waves
and wandering spirits
quite unable to tell them apart

They would not be Moved!

The men of Petite Savane refusing
to leave their evacuated village
claimed they were justified in staying put
until they had eaten every last one of their fine pigs.
So daily, they cooked up a storm,
broth made of succulent pork chops
and tasty dasheens from their well-tended gardens.
But what if the rains returned?
If the rivers rose from their temporary torpor
to display their rage afresh?
And what if the men grew fat,
too large, too slow and altogether too unfit
to wrestle with new floods?
What then?
They didn't care.
They only knew that this was one sure way
of defying too cruel Nature
of getting their own back.
And so against all protestations, they stayed.

Barbecued Cow

Don't eat dead animals, the health bulletins warned
- a message which could have carried weight
when words such as "contamination", "infection", "disease"
still held fear inducing powers.
But those were not ordinary times,
when an arid public road could be transformed into a raging torrent.
Those were no ordinary times, when a living room
full to the brim with rising water became a death trap
snatching in its claws grandfather and toddler;
and those were no ordinary times
as a hitherto healthy heifer
someone's carefully tended livelihood
now floated ponderously downstream, destined to go to waste.
Well, instinctively the people dragged her from the flood
and with sharp knives proceeded to cut off slices
which they roasted on open fires
and with grim satisfaction thereby assuaged their hunger.
The traumatised girl from Hackney, London
wet clothes clinging to her slight, shivering frame
though hungry and by no means a squeamish vegetarian
decided that the only steak to cross her lips
would be one with the supermarket's plastic seal.

Nature

Sunset over the Bay

When the sun prepares to bed down for the night
a flurry of creatures big and small
gather round to pay homage to the empress of all light
basking in the final moments of her warm glow.
Their enigmatic shapes hover like shadow puppets
against a luminous, crimson backdrop.
Those pictures, ever changing, from gambolling lambs
to horse-drawn carriage at break-neck speed,
sometimes a playful puppy chasing its own tail
or a nascent bird clinging to an invisible branch.
At times it's as if a painter, on washing his brushes
had carelessly flung the multi-coloured effluence
to drip-drop across the horizon.
Indulgently, the sun beams upon her faithful servants
then lowering her lashes and pinching her nose
she glides into rapid and complete emersion.
The ethereal creatures, their ministrations done,
drift off with little more ado
into the darkness and the night.

Small Things

Once in every while
something brushes past the edges of my imagination
leaving it to ponder the power of small things, random and rare.

Take the four chicks, coal-black, encircling a snow-white mother hen
grubbing with the rhythm and precision of an African dance
one step forwards, scratch, scratch, scratch
one step backwards, swing, scratch, scratch;
evidence of kinship elusive, until the barely visible specks of ebony
sparsely adorning her tail, hint at a genetic connection.

Before sunrise on another day,
swathed in orange, pink and blue, with fading bands of red,
a crescent moon lay in repose, a milky saucer for her bed.
That rainbow was indeed short-lived,
three blinks, a passing cloud and it was gone;
but etched deep in my memory, that masterpiece lives on.

What of the ephemeral iridescent arc, stretching skywards,
high above a congested London street, far from its lowly birthing bed
of effluence from exhaust pipes, drizzly rain and weak sunlight
to emerge an exquisite rainbow, daring in its unexpectedness.

A world away from rainbows in Wanstead Park, one summer's day,
a mother swan advanced
picture of serenity, gliding majestically,
a ship with alabaster sails unfurled,
admired by strollers on the banks of Heron Lake,
a welcome distraction from the incessant barking
of an irksome little dog, who alas did not see the swan approach
could not have foreseen his punishment by drowning.
In consternation gasped the crowd
as the owner to no avail hurled his sticks and protestations.

My final prize must be bestowed upon the grimy, once-white jalopy
trundling along the bumpy track to Dominica's Donkey Beach

proudly proclaiming itself "Coral Reef on Wheels",
a touch of irony too delicious not to have
painted a smile across the thinnest lips,
raised a song in the coldest heart, and
a most hearty cheer to the god of small things.

In Wanstead Park, Notice!

There will be
no bathing
no boating
no swimming
nor fishing
in the Shoulder of Mutton Pond

Dip your toes if you want to
catch a swan if you can
but please
no bathing
no boating
no swimming
nor fishing
in the Shoulder of Mutton Pond

For hours on end
you can stand and stare
stroke a goose if you dare
but be warned
there must be no bathing,
no boating
no swimming
nor fishing
in the Shoulder of Mutton Pond

You may day-dream if you wish
or watch the young coots
as with grace and panache
they gambol and fish
but absolutely
no bathing
no boating
no swimming
nor fishing
in the Shoulder of Mutton Pond

You may dilly-dally and dawdle
oh yes, even kiss and cuddle
tell tall tales like Anancy
frisk and frolic if you fancy
but remember
no bathing
no boating
no swimming
nor fishing
in the enticing waters
of the Shoulder of Mutton Pond.

Mini Volcano

My stomach is a volcano, dormant until disturbed
where a drink of water will turn innocent air bubbles
into summersaulting burps and heartburn.

An enjoyable meal will produce a paroxysm of churning
clawing, growling, gnawing, rumbling and belching
loud enough to wake the mermaid of the Boiling Lake

Some of those bubbles shoot upwards like hissing geysers
while others volubly inhabit the nethermost regions
indelicately exiting whenever they must.

At times, my stomach could be a somnolent snake, tightly coiled
until, sprinkled with droplets or pellets
it shivers and stirs in a ponderous gremlin's dance.

Oh for the kindly expertise of Doctor Kapoor
in locating the source of my reptilian volcano
and blasting it clean away!

Cool Beat

Hear the sea roar, as it flings itself against the shore
Feel the wind blow, as it ruffles your reflection in streams that glow
Smell the sun's heat, as it tingles every nerve
of your desire to surrender to the joy of life
without cold feet

Be a devil
On the level with your nothingness
Be a victor
Live and conquer this nagging urge to sink
beneath the burden of your nothingness

Mock the sea's strength
Breathe the wind's cool
Soak the sun's warmth
and mould your heart
into a raft of endurance that rides calm
even as storms rage all around you
Match life's insanity
with your immunity from breaking into sweat
keeping a cool, cool beat
on this narrow, rugged street.

Night Lady

Impatiently she nudges the setting sun
intent on hastening the hour of her rising.
Admiring her reflection in an albinotic lake
she glides off on many a sinister mission.
Irritated by the smugness of a calm sea
she might spit out unruly pips of truculence
to heave and crash against the somnolent shore.
She could, if she so wished
rudely intrude upon the near-intimacy
of two platonic friends
and with one sting of Eros' blistering breath
turn them into hapless lovers.
Her favourite pastime is to hover past the open window of an asylum
whose inmates, petrified by her lurid presence
stir uneasily in tortured sleep.
Always, the moon smiles with maternal affinity
for her spellbound lunatics
darkly binding them to her milky bosom.

Chanson D'Amour

Qu'elle est belle
Ma petite île aux Antilles
Qu'elle est fraîche
Qu'elle est douce!

Parée de hautes montagnes
De milles collines
Et dans ce manteau de verdure
Qui l'enveloppe des quatre coins
Qu'elle est bien!

Sans cesse siffle son vent
Ses bois dansent en chantant
Ses fleurs poussent sans gêne
Une beauté qui touche le coeur
Qui inspire un amour libre, sans peine
Qu'elle est jeune!

Et ses gens sympathiques
Amoureux de la vie
Qu'ils sont gais
Qu'ils sont braves
Généreux, courageux
Même un peu paresseux
Qu'ils sont beaux!

Et quand je suis a l'étranger
Qu'elles me manquent
Les eaux chaudes des Caraïbes
Je me meurs de respirer de nouveau
L'odeur de la terre toute tiède
Toute fumante
Du mariage de pluie et chaleur.

La Dominique, île de mangues et d'ananas
Je t'embrasse!

Love

The Odd Couple

he likes coffee, she prefers tea
her game is netball, his cricket
he adores children, she loathes brats
she hates window shopping, he loves browsing
she listens to Radio 4, ooh, ya, he tunes in to Ragga FM, iree!
he is a Coronation Street fan, give her East Enders any day
she finds Sainsbury's good value indeed, he favours Waitrose for
   quality appeal
she needs red meat for her pernicious anaemia
he must eat white for his too high cholesterol
he takes a cool, brisk shower in the morning
she lingers in a warm bubble bath in the evening
he prefers the bedroom cool, she turns up the thermostat
well, she rolls to the right
he faces the wall to the left
deep Red-Sea cleft in the middle
until someone makes the first move
the other relents
together they consent
and the rest, as they say
is love history

Talk to me of Love

Talk to me of love and I recall the rainbow you invented
to beguile the sun one rainy day
but your rainbow proved alas, not colourfast
and so stained before fading into mist
the patchwork dream I'd weaved around my hopes

Talk to me of love and you conjure up tropical rain
beating frenziedly upon a hot zinc roof
those raindrops do cause a quickening in the veins
before I yield to cosy somnolence
when rudely halts the pattering rain
and with it, my pleasant languor down the drain

Talk to me of love and I'll paint you an illusion
a Dominican night viewed from the porch
of a house high on the hill
magical night, wild almond scented
tinged with coffee blossoms and salt sea spray
extolled by a million stars
flaunting their reflection on a sleepy sea
mimicked by a masquerade of dancing fireflies
mutely mocking the fool who would possess a Dominican night

Make Hay while the Sun Shines

By chance we met one summer's day
How long we've got I cannot say
Suffice that we did meet and found
a mutual attraction
with added friendship which we hope
will stand the test of time

Why dwell on future rifts
on shapeless dreams
love's cruel stings or bitter disappointments?
Let's love and live each precious day
that if tomorrow never comes
at least we know we've had today

Love's Touch

Love grew one summer
Blossomed through winter
Faded in spring and by late autumn
had surrendered its lifeless petals
to the winds of change

Fear Not my Love

Please do not ask me to deny nor to explain
the deep affection I bear you
for it has no beginning

Time stands forever still while life glides past
the open windows of our hearts
A moving kaleidoscope
revealing landscapes unpredictable
in complex shades of human emotion

One day the tableau drifting by was you
Too soon it will have gone
Tonight, if only you could smile
And we were less afraid.

Memories for Valentine's Day

Valentine's Day is almost gone
No chocolates, no cards, no flowers for Agnes
But does she sit down and weep, lie prostrate and wail? Hell, no!
With the thickest, richest slice of carrot cake from Stratford's
    indoor market,
she curls up beneath her duvet and tucks in.
The first bite doesn't disappoint; it melts upon the tongue
lifting her as on the crest of an oceanic wave.
The taste of nutmeg, cinnamon and ginger of the second bite
evokes one of those splendid, crimson sunsets
lingering over Grand Bay every evening at 6 pm precisely.
By the time she's polished off the last crumb
she's right there with her mum in the carnival band
clutching the protective hand, gingerly swaying.
Eyes now tight-shut, she is whisked to a place
where spellbound, she listened to tales by moonlight
of tricksters Brer Rabbit and Anancy, up to no good, as usual.
Thus sated and soothed, she falls asleep that Valentine's
    afternoon
to the hypnotic rhythms of tropical rain.
Casting off her light clothing, she dips her toes
in the crystal waters of River Montine
there to bathe and bask once again
in the sun-drenched, skinny-dipping innocence of childhood.

Cupid's Bow

Once in a while something stumbles uninvited
onto the canvas of your consciousness
Once in a while needle-sharp tingles vibrate past your inner
   landscape
shattering the serenity you had so carefully cradled there
Once in a while you sense a gazing into your soul
a disturbing, bitter-sweet intrusion
Once in every while, such a phantom does appear
to stoke up the embers of your imaginings
Causing its dimly remembered heart beat to quicken and resound
Once in a while, this intruder will catch you unawares
as you inhale his aphrodisiac charms.

Once in a while when it duly drifts your way, pure panic may ensue
as confidence caving in, you quiver in your solitude
secretly savouring the despair of an ugly duckling
in the presence of her prince of swans

Once in a while, amid the hazy merging of fantasy with harsh reality
It's small comfort, yet still comforting to know
that cupid, for all his cross-eyed clumsiness
may aim in your direction, if only for a while
once in every while.

To Life

You are the mountain, you are the sea
You are the butterfly floating free

You are the hummingbird, you are the bee
Plucking sweet nectar from a heliconia tree

You are the rain, you are the sun
Holding hands together for rainbow fun

You are the wind, you are the breeze
Maker of music for sentient trees

You are the pulse, you are the beat
Of tropical rhythms beneath my feet

You are the sky, you are the ground
From east to west, let beauty abound

You are Day, you are Night
Embracing Creation with infinite might

Tangled Web

Seek not your liberation in your lover's eyes
for this crystal pool you see is not the medium
by which you shall be free
it will but draw you like a whirlpool
into the vortex of his fears
his insecurity
inadequacy
mediocrity
his uncertainty
mendacity
his all too stunted capacity to give
and when you have assumed his lot
and as from a daydream you wake
from that sublime delusion
he'll only squint and looking vacant
will slowly turn his gaze upon
the next mobile object
while the luminous pool recedes
leaving an ashy residue
a dry, sawdusty bilious after-taste
instead, look to yourself, delve deep
to fight your own battles, win your goals
unearth your hidden magic
but don't, for goodness sake
seek your fortune in your lover's eye
or you'll be beamed a lie

Dissonance

Neocolonisation

my country is a polka dot reclining on two oceans
my country is an emerald pool between two Francophone lands
Wai'tukubuli my country
tall her body
as her Kalinago name proclaims
Wai'-tu-ku-buli
Wai'-tu-ku-buli
Wai'-tu-ku-buli
Why do I still today
hear such strong echoes of invader drums?
I run my fingers up the ridges of her spine
to rest on Trois Pitons
three peaks that jot out solemnly
with eyes that moisten with sulphuric tears
for our Nature Isle, now quite prostrate
before the exalted US dollar
in no need of permission
to plant its conqueror's progress flag
upon the tombs of obesity
imported with Subway and KFC
my country's but a dot
where dreams of beauty, luxury and love
immodestly gyrate to the rhythms of American soaps
whose operas stomp across her shores
from dot to blinking, flickering, blinkered dot

Allies

with friends like you, what fear of enemies?
to speak to me in riddles for which you're dubbed articulate
then deem me unintelligent when I fail to comprehend
is to cheat just as your forefathers did
when they dangled glittery brass before my ancestors
while plucking in exchange the golden etchings from their souls.
for I know full well that your heart's an empty vessel
which shuns the cargo of my cares
do me a favour and hold your peace
while I fathom for myself the mysteries of life
let me consort only with those whose eyes reflect
an unspoken understanding
more eloquent than your thousand words
so glibly tripping from false tongue
and even colder heart.

Change, what Change?

change is as change does
but the arbiters of change
have they sufficiently analysed
its whys and wherefores?
have they full cognisance of its aftermath
and do they even care?
In sleep, it's good to dream
to change the world
on waking, it's even sweeter to remember
but spare us the tunnel visions
of those who would not just transform
but seek to subjugate the universe

Drowning the Silence

when silence speaks louder than words
it's time to attune the inner ear
to the sound of unarticulated fear
when spoken word is replaced by stifled sighs
respectful dialogue a lost art
verbal communication too casually dismissed
in favour of crisp memos
eye contact furtive, speaking volumes
body language uneasy, taut
then it must be time to confront head on this malaise
time to fling open wide the windows, letting fresh air in
time to reconstruct the art of self-belief
and were we then to breathe in unison
could not the ensuing heartbeat
resound loud enough
to drown the silence and the rats?

Creole's Plea

I want to go to de ball tonight
I want to go to de language ball
where de words so sweet
an de music nice
an meaning is served with a touch of spice
where verb come without auxiliary
where plural appear only where it please
an adverb replacing verb with ease
I want to go to de ball tonight
I want to go to de language ball
where present and past tense
dancing to de same drum beat
with preposition coming to de rescue
lest confusion ensue
word ending and article
sure to be out on sabbatical
but those twin bouncers bound to be there
prefix limbering up to take de floor
suffix smartly bringing up the rear

I want to go to de ball tonight
I want to go so bad
but I hear dey having audition
to see who have impeccable pronunciation
they checking for grammar and syntax and ting
to see who can best speak de language of de Queen
man, when de alphabet prince come round
to find de lingo of he dream
I know things going to go all wrong
as wicked step mudder won't want me aroun
so between me an you
I secretly prime up parrot
to help me in three different tongue
La plie belle en bas la baye
De nicest one hiding under de tub

The most beautiful lies hidden under the wash tub
but if I know dat bird
he'll get in a right mix-up
when parrot fashion he try to speak all three
an where will dat leave me, hein?
I ask you, where will dat leave me?

Waiting

We are sitting
here in the dark
waiting for the dawn
to lift our burdens
roll away our pain
but we have been waiting so long
we suffer the heartburn
of undigested hope
of undreamed dreams
instead of dawn
inertia comes creeping in
put close upon by paralysis
both fat and sleek
from little people's misery
although, they say
the darkest hour is before the dawn
good things come to those who wait
and joy cometh in the morning
let us wait no more
but rise and meet the dawn
clear eyed and unafraid
to reclaim the dignity
that is so rightly ours

Cuts

The residents came in and sat down
hope, like a fluttering pigeon
struggling, despite their droopy shoulders
to flicker in their eyes
as they waited for the Leader

but the man from local government
strode up to the rostrum
clipped, masterful gait
arched eyebrows
boding no compromise
a few curt announcements later
and he sallied out again

like mute mourners at a graveside
the crowd dispersed
home to a cup of tea
a glass of warmed up Norfolk punch
perhaps even a thimbleful of Scotch
while they could still afford it

Affirmation

through the tunnels of history
you stooped
trekked
trudged
submerged but never sunk
you endured load upon your head
yoke around your neck
weight upon your shoulders
chains around hands and feet and loins
hot iron on your skin
deep lacerations to your soul
through all of this you have emerged hurt
and scared
a great deal scarred
but still fully upright
and will you tell me now
that you've forgotten how to smile
your spirit can no longer soar
your heart has lost the zest to sing
with tongue that cannot bless your race
that those same hands dare not create
your feet a stranger to the dance
your body a mere shell
that you've forgotten how to live and love?
I tell you now, I cannot, will not believe you
for I was there and got to know you far too well

Black Vote

It may be just a cross to you, to me it is dignity
It may be just the letter X to you, to me it is liberty
It may be just a black mark on white paper to you
but for the Black Majority
It meant reclaiming from Apartheid its humanity

If the dead could speak
a million voices would rise
to greet the hoisting of this new flag
If the dead could speak
the tongues of sacrificial lambs
for peace and justice everywhere would loosen
to proclaim their songs of praise
along with all the heroes and sheroes
whose blood was spilt for freedom

It may be just a cross to you, to us it's liberation
It may be the letter X to you, to us it is the key to reparation
It may be but a black mark on paper to you
but to us it is the starting post

It may be the symbol of democracy elsewhere
but here, it's much, much greater
for it is signature in blood by those present
for them absent

It may be just a cross to you
the letter X
a black mark on white paper
but to us it is testimony of our endurance
our survival
our triumph of the human spirit

So it may be just a cross to you
the letter X
a black mark on white paper
maybe just a black mark on white paper to you
but to us it signifies pure black on white
for what is right

Making Poverty History

Once, there was a mouse who wished to help a lion in a cage
wanted to set him free, as lions ought to be
so she gnawed till her gums were raw
chewed till her teeth were sore
and do you know, in the end
the little mouse, she set that awesome creature free?

Once there was a bloodthirsty giant
who terrorised a village in the middle of the plains
countless brave men pitted their strength but failed
until one day, a fearless youth took up his bow
and aiming high
struck his arrow right between the target's eye

Once there were church halls and sundry places across the land
full of people gathered to imagine a world
where everyone could live
fresh air, clean water, jobs
and all things life-sustaining
and did it happen, this modern miracle?
Perhaps not yet
but while there are those in our midst
still inspired and able to dream
there is hope

Exile's Running Dream

another dawn
a slate-grey sunrise
I lie stock still
trying to recapture
the fragile threads
of my night's dreaming
where I drift along the White River
evoke once again the mountain whistler
whose song has never ceased
to haunt my daydreams.
I pass the time
undoing stitch by stitch
those frayed edges of my life
into a serpentine carpet
amidst which, green shoots
tangled in mangroves
and dank seaweed
sprout here and there
soon to be smothered
in the careless embraces
of a random tide

Failed Friendship

often it's hard
to lay one's finger
on exactly why
one is out of step
with the dance of life
hard to ascertain
why cracks appear
to blur the vision
with lengthening shadows
where sunlight should abound

where doubts loom large
good intentions flounder
then fade away
leaving a wistful longing
for something that might have been
a new friendship
perhaps left unexplored
and lost forever

Twice orphaned

to love so well
care that much
try too hard
while surrogate mother
unrequiting
indicates in a thousand ways
just how much
her font of unconditional love
runs over
not for me
was never mine to claim
and this I must concede
has cut more deeply
than when first
I was bereaved

Poison Ivy

on bandy legs she creeps around
strange daughter of the house
she'll come upon you unawares
as quiet as a mouse
on thin bow legs she creeps about
this daughter of the house
you'll catch her listening in at keyholes
loathsome as a louse

Birthday Lament

so depressed
sherry in the afternoon
blurred contours of the mind
so depressed
another birthday
edging perilously close
to the brink of menopause

so depressed
men
or lack of them
oh pause
and take a hard look
into your emptied glass
so depressed
your face a picture
of things as they ought not

so depressed
enough to sink without a trace
but one drop more
a long, deep sleep
and the sun will rise regardless
as it always does
from somewhere in the east.

Blizzard

February 1969, New York
when a mini-skirted girl stumbles
onto the slippery tarmac at JFK
her thin cotton shawl pulled tight
a three-day blizzard
a city under siege
as a sea of unaccustomed whiteness
assails her in the manner of those gargantuan waves
from the ocean back home
with force enough to toss many a daring swimmer
into oblivion
she struggles to stay on her feet
as below zero temperatures clutch at her breath
squeezing it out in spirals of white smoke
which hang mid-air as delicate icicles
mounds of snow inhabit the sidewalks
like ghoulish albatrosses frozen in time
or ghostly one-eyed night watchmen in a sci-fi movie

the dazzling blue sky, hitherto a cordial friend
now bears down with naked hostility, closing in upon her
she is a tropical flower withering in the grip of icy tentacles
taking another cautious breath
she draws herself up to her full height
gird your loins, my girl
no promise of warm springs here for you

Vacancy

your room stands bare
stripped as it is of those erotic posters
which served so well
to hide the starkness of imperfect walls
looks bare
devoid of your garments
discarded helter-skelter
across unmade bed
like a shy maiden
caught unawares undressed
and endeavouring with scant success
to preserve her modesty
the smell of absence more pungent now
than your odoriferous aftershave
and socks rolled up
in little balls about the floor
life's a bit like that and yet...
was it truly that hard
to mumble a few words of thanks
or even just 'goodbye'?

Praise

For Estelle Elmechali

Write me a ditty
Sing me a song
Coo me a lullaby
To make me strong

Tell me a story
From days of old
Weave it in colours
Red, green and bold

Woo me with melody
Notes I can reach
Touch me with inspiration
That I may teach

Sing to me fervently
A sharing song
Rock me so gently
Let me know I belong

Song for Rachele

Come generous heart
Ever loving, thoughtful and kind
Caring for others always on your mind

If you were a hummingbird
A gentle shower of rain
If you were a rainbow over meadow or plain
We couldn't love you more, dear Rachele

If you were a full moon
Pouring your silvery light
On Pete, Mum and Macy and everyone so bright
We couldn't love you more, dear Rachele

We salute you London girl
We salute you Dominican belle
For your winning ways and the things you do so well
Know that we love you so, dear Rachele

To The Unknown Biker

6th October, 1997
Dear Editor,
If you could spare the space for these few lines
I would be ever so grateful:

Somewhere out there is a biker
who he is I'll never know
but be he Mod or be he Rocker
I would like to name him Hero

I have kept this bit of paper
which he left upon my car
to remind me of his good deed
and the fact that he was there

My plea for help was tentative
as spluttering, my car went dead
but he rose to the occasion
helped me push, then took control

Safely parked, I walked away
to a phone and the AA
but on my return, oh no!
stuck to my windscreen...

Phew! not the dreaded ticket but... a cardboard shield
in wobbly capitals emblazoned
BROKEN DOWN. GONE FOR HELP

I could have wept from sheer relief
and the thoughtfulness of the man
whoever and wherever he may be
would you please say a big THANK YOU
from me?

Yours faithfully
Ms Jane U Grell
9 Lyttelton Road
London E10 5NQ

In conversation with the late Tony Lee

So tell us, Tony Lee
What are you up to now, hein?
No doubt fund-raising, talent-scouting
Appraising your umpteenth rehearsal
in some draughty celestial youth club
or community centre?
Could you perhaps be lobbying hard
as only you knew how
an arts committee, town council
an executive for youth affairs
a college bursar?
We wouldn't put it past you

With never a moment to yourself
you mentored troubled youth
helped them discover hidden talents
your determination legendary
unshakeable as a limpet

Like a free-flowing river
your energy was boundless
a veritable aqueduct
filtering the dreams of so many
for so long and in so many ways

So rest in peace, dear brother
assured that memories of you are circling still
beyond Waltham Forest
way over the Thames
and across the globe

Rest in peace and know that while you sleep
Estate of the Arts lives on
busy "getting down"

Woman

Stand back
Well back
This woman is about to self-destruct
Thirty second flat
Truth is,
She's tired of being
The quintessence of
Strength
Sense
Hope
The comforter
Tired of having to be
Cool
Calm
Collected
Unruffled
Even when her walls are caving in
Tired of demands for miracles
To prove her womanhood

Don't advance
She isn't bluffing
Not this time
She's tired of having to leap over
The hundred and one obstacles
Strewn in her path everyday
To trap her
While you strain her will
And pull down her defences
She's tired of having to suppress her desires
With never a taste of the honeyed gall
That's yours for the taking
Tired of having to submit
While screaming protest silently
Recoiling

Tired of being earth mother
The Madonna whose fountain of unconditional love
Is drained relentlessly by you
Pleading weakness privately
While publicly exuding confidence
In claiming your self-awarded birthright
Of having your cake and eating it too

This woman is about to self-destruct
Watch out! Her fuse is almost spent
The sparks are about to fly any moment now
Don't try to soothe her; too late
She's done with bribery
Doesn't believe in the sincerity of your pleas
Your pathetic apologies
She will not be placated by empty promises
As she's been duped too many times before

Do her one last favour
And give her the space she needs
To lick her wounds better
And survive the onslaught
Of just how far your music of discord
Is out of tune with her desire
To do the dance of life
On this grisly tombstone
Which you would allot her

Woman of Words

I am a woman of words
Ordinary words
Sometimes sad
Never bad
No rude words
I am a woman of words
Fine words
Compassionate
Never empty words
I seldom have precise words
Find it quite hard to be concise
I am no Oxford Dictionary
Yet, I am a woman of words
Old hat words
Like, Tom drunk, Tom no fool
Wise, me granny-used-to-say words
Chile, you'll make a beautiful woman, you know, but later
Calm the fear inside, comforting words

I am a woman of words
Bold, direct and unafraid words
Down with the Tories, cha!
I am a woman of words
Bilingual
Kweyol and creole words
Mwem cay yon femme plein mots
Bel ti mots kweyol
Bon ti mots, ou tanne
Pas piece gwos mots, awah
Mwem femme cela ni mots pour charme' ou
Pour touche' cher ou, aie, aie, aie
Parle' mwem di ca doux-doux mwen

I am a woman of words
Chosen words
Sometimes no words at all

I don't need words to tell you what I think of you
One smile, one sweet eye
Can say it all
One cheups, one cut eye
That's you summed up
So who needs words?
Still... perhaps just a few
After all, a woman of words
Still needs her small comforts

Song of the Ugly Duckling

I never was good-looking
I guess I'll never be
but the knowledge that I'm beautiful
is comforting to me

Good looks come as a dowry
given free at birth
beauty is gleaned
from tuning in to the music of your heart-strings
composing your own symphony
to aid surefootedness
along life's uneven road

No one has told me lately
I guess they just can't see
but the knowledge that I'm beautiful
is like a balm to me

To Manijeh

A little worm blinked nervously
in the presence of an unaccustomed light.
Come said the torch, gently beckoning
I've got a task in hand for you.
Me, gulped the little wizened one in disbelief,
retreating
What can I do?
Ah, that depends on you
smiled the lady tantalising, her dancing orbs
infusing a daring glow into the little form
that sent it reeling with, for the first time
a sense of its own something-ness
Then followed a desire
for the need to shout
"I am more than just a worm!"
What joy!
What boundless ecstasy!
No apology
strictly first persons, I and me.
Now, to whom it may concern
please let it be known that I am a butterfly
a bird
tomorrow a rattlesnake
I will not crawl or squirm, nor wriggle or stutter
I'll choose to ripple or sting
fly or flutter, as I please.

And always, always
will I hold her in my gaze
that shiny beacon, fearless
and beautiful exceedingly

Moko Jumbie

Moko Jumbie walks tall
a magnificent rainbow-god on stilts.
From a perilous height,
moving in staccato to the haunting beat
of African drums, steel pans and jing-ping bands.
Swathed in the rhythms of two worlds entwined,
from the tribes of Congo
the Igbos and Yorubas of Niger
to the pulsating carnival streets
of Antigua, Dominica, Grenada, Trinidad...
Moko Jumbie, indefatigable dancer,
wise diviner,
protector of the people
guardian of the indomitable spirit
of children of Africa, for almost four hundred years
crushed but not cremated,
damaged but not dead,
exiled but not extinct;
a timeless colossus and mythical African godhead
stepping in time
to the gyrations of liberated Antillean ghosts.
Moko Jumbie, symbol incarnate
of survival against all odds.

The Poem Lady

Are you the poem lady?
this volunteer mum greeted me
in the school corridor one day
on my way to my poetry workshop
with a class of eleven year olds.
- my calabash and rain-stick must have given me away
Yes, I smiled, a bit tongue tied
but rather pleased and flattered
by the title *poem lady*
Keep on doing what you doing, she continued, approvingly
My PJ was never one for poems, but now he can't stop writing
They don't always rhyme and that, but he tries so hard
He says, the poem lady's coming tomorrow
and we all get to read our poems

I have never forgotten this spontaneous display
of parental appreciation
so now, before every poetry workshop
I offer grateful thanks to all the PJs of this world
along with their mums and teachers
I remember too the other poem women and men
of long ago, known and unknown
and those living today
who continue to inspire and enthral
with their music of words

Grandmother's Armchair

So this is it then, Chair, the end
where we part company, you and I?
True, you squint and dribble piteously
a poor lame has-been
maimed from the brunt of a lifetime's sitting
a home to bugs and fleas
yet, my Aladdin's lamp, no replacement ever!
for only you can whisk me back years
over seas, across miles
to a place where nights were star-spangled and warm
a puppy at my grandmother's feet
curled up at the foot of her chair while she rocked
waiting for stories to roll off her tongue
like infant waves upon a pebbled beach, tireless, hypnotic.
Now you, oh chair, her final keepsake
have done your time and I must let you go,
but not to a rubbish dump.
Instead, I'll pile your mangled frame sky high
upon this funeral pyre whose rapid flames shall, while consuming
release your spirit and hers into the stratosphere
as dormant echoes that spring to life whenever someone treads
be it ever so lightly upon her memory

Celebration

Perennial Prayer

Oh for a little time!
Time to trust
Dream dreams
Hope.
Time to show courage in the face of pain
Death
Life.

Time to be touched by peace
Joy
Love,
Time...
Enough to grow
to know
Myself
You
The other
Just a little better

Poetry Cohoblopot

I am sitting here, in this chair
wondering what the weather
must be like in Dominica.
Quit daydreaming!
This voice kicks viciously from underneath the table of my
      conscience;
then yet another nudge
Deal with the task in hand!
Ok, Ok, I'll write... I'll write a poem
But do I really have to?
I suck on the nib of my Parker pen
Shall it be *how to write a poem*?
Old hat
It has been done countless times before.
How to eat a poem?
That too has been folded and put to bed.
Maybe something a tad more off the wall?
Like, first gather randomly a bunch of words
toss into a cohoblopot
marinade in wild-word juice
then shake well with some noun-encrusted adjectives
sprinkled with a few adverbial droplets.
Squeeze the mixture through the sluggish breath
of a just-about-to-rise imagination
and with a little perseverance, who knows?
it could emerge
perhaps not gourmet yet a perfectly edible poetry treat.

In 2046

they came from miles
they travelled far
they came on foot
by bus, by car
they gathered round
they sat them down
upon the floor
on pouffes, chairs
and intently listened
to the storyteller's soothing voice
no practised oratory
no firebrand preacher's style had she
nor talk of revolution
just a soft meandering medley
of this and that.
Are you a singer? One of them asked
after she'd led them in a ballad
You could say that, she smiled
Are you a poet? Queried another
as she spun a web of words
through which she blew speech bubbles
roguishly
perhaps, she said in dreamy tones
Are you a storyteller too?
Oh, I do hope so
was her prompt reply
You play children's games as well
interposed another
What kind of grown up are you?
If you are so full of scorn
then tell me, why did you come?
Our televisions are defunct
computer systems have all crashed
they said you were an internet alternative
albeit a little primitive.

It seemed to the storyteller
that they were not far wrong
eyes brimming over with the truth of it.
They walked away in single file
no hand-outs did they clutch
no apps, no printouts
nothing but a warming glow
left by the rhythm of a clapping game
the cadence of a poem
while stories like beads of pearl
threaded through the hairlines
of their imagination.

They came from far
they came from near
they left at length in pouring rain
a fitting backdrop
to the storyteller's stentorian refrain.

Yard Talk

Odysseas! Odysseas! Odys-se-as!
Boy, you don't hear me calling you? Whey there you is?
Chut! The whole of L'allee have to hear my voice, so early in the
   morning
Just come here lemme cut your tail for you,
sacre ti potance, you likkle good-for-nothing
Lord, you seeing my cross with that boy, oui
With his vie jamme kambwe and bond mate
is not likkle rude, that boy rude, non
Satis zie kokliche, ti piciette
You think is likkle talk he making me talk?
So whey you been since morning eh, Mister Man
Odysseas, is manish you playing mannish?
What? Papa Bondie, give me strength
Odysseas, me Mavis, zenfant Ma Paul
Send you to interfere with mr Nassief coconut
Right where it is on his estate?
Well if you cyan hear, you must feel
And if you dosen understand English
Then I'll have to give it to you in kweyol
Odysseas, come here lemme haler your zorweille, you running?
Lemme ketch you and see if I don fan your chu, for true
An defonce you too
Zor, the boy laughing you know, so now, I is his papyshow?
Odysseas, boy come here lemme kill you
Odysseas, ti garcon, veni ici por mwem chewe ou
Ou las vive!

Good Riddance

I lay within a foaming bath
and soaked my cares away
all my burdens came rolling off
in little lumps of grey

One big bubble clung to my back
I shrugged it off with ease
Would you believe it? – my old school
I said: "Be gone now, if you please!"

The great big bubble rolled away
and landed on my toe
I wiggled viciously to kill
my long established foe

The bubble blinked in disbelief
Could I indeed be free?
I prodded hard with my big toe
the bubble squirmed with misery

It went out grudgingly, without a sound
done, gone, forgotten
to you, great hulking Upton House
am I no longer bound

Bloodlines

An adolescent girl looks on amazed
as the uncle whom she has only just met
speaks, throws back his head and laughs
morphing before her very eyes into her granddad

A young woman's heart lurches
as through a half-open door
she observes her grandmother pensively loosening her hair
In that moment, it is none other than her mother she sees sitting there

This little boy, presented for the first time to his great grandmother
initially recoils
One hesitant hug later and he seems somehow reassured
that they must have met somewhere before

The middle-aged woman, orphaned in childhood
consumed by yearning
confides her deep regret that not one photograph exists
as testimony that her mother did exist

Just look in the mirror, her confidante advised
and so one day, tweaking out an errant grey hair or two
while contemplating her reflection
she could have sworn she saw her mother wink
and felt strangely comforted

Earnest Invitation

Attempting to cross a busy road in Leyton, one day
Eyes peeled on traffic dancing past on deadly wheels
When suddenly, from somewhere a shrill call
Miss Gr – i –I - l!

I pirouetted round, a trifle startled, but then on seeing it was a
    schoolboy
Nodded and with an instinctive, oh hello, faking a bright smile
to cover up my lack of recognition.

This is where I live, that road, the caller informed me
pointing to an undistinguished row of terraced houses
Right, I agreed and hoped I sounded interested.
Erskine Road, number 23, he continued with precision.
That's nice, I nodded absently, knowing I would instantly forget.
You can come to my house tomorrow, he offered, unexpectedly.
Are you inviting me? I asked, just to make things quite clear, you
    understand.
Yes, come tonight, was his unequivocal reply.

This was unmistakably a dinner invitation for which I was amused
    and touched.
Cheeky monkey, I thought. His mum would have a thing or two to
    say about that,
I shouldn't wonder
Then and there, I decided to call his bluff, the little blighter

Picture the scene:
Knock, knock on the door of number 23 Erskine Road.
Door slowly opens and I'm greeted by a puzzled, kindly face
Yes?
Mrs Ilyas?
Yes?
We haven't met but I'm one of Khuram's teachers.
An anxious cloud dims her eyes before she enquires: Khuram in
    trouble?

No, no, Khuram's a very nice boy. He's in no trouble at all.
I'm here because he's invited me to dinner.
Dinner? What dinner?
She didn't mean to sound so brusque and I completely
    understood.
Deciding it best to compromise a little, I offered to come another
    day
If it's not convenient, I started, back-tracking
No, no, come in, come in, there's plenty dinner
Her voice now both convincing and sincere.
I half melt into the mouth-watering aroma
wafting from the kitchen
greatly tempted to shut out the evening cold
and the crazy crush of rush hour traffic.

But wait, hang on
I was the teacher, full of sound sense, I hear you rightly say
and the boy Khuram? Well, only full of innocence and youthful
    generosity
So kind of you, Khuram. Another day, I'll come another day, I lied,
    recklessly.
OK, Miss, Ba – aye!
Blessing his impetuous heart
I dived dangerously, Wonder Woman style, between two whizzing
    cars,
on no greater mission than a trip to the greengrocer's
to buy fresh okras for my fish curry.

Unbridled Joy

Laughing woman found running, naked.
Running woman found naked, laughing.
Naked woman found laughing, running.
Found running naked, laughing woman.
Laughing, naked woman found running.
Naked, laughing, running; woman found.
Laughing, running, naked, found woman.
Woman found! Naked, running, laughing.

Christmas Eve

Christmas Eve – Delices

The haunting strains of an accordion band
the newly-scraped gleaming red earth of the yard,
the colourful strip of brand new linoleum adorning the wooden
floor
the pervasive smell of freshly slaughtered pork roasting upon the
coal-pot
Yes, Christmas had come

The village bathed in moonlight,
a country road with ghostly shadows dancing
the thump-thumping of hurrying feet to midnight mass
urged on by the pealing bells

No Christmas tree or well-wrapped presents,
perhaps a top or tin whistle for the boys
a skinny six-penny doll, fragile in her nakedness,
on whose behalf we girls scavenged discarded bits of cloth
in an effort to redeem her modesty.

Back home from midnight mass, we feasted on beef soup
and gorged on sweets bought with our precious pennies.
Some of us stole a sip of cherry brandy from an indulgent grown-
up's glass,
sheer bliss, matched only by the pleasure of drifting off to sleep
to the crooning of a lone carolling minstrel,
serenading every house in the hope of food and drink;
and if lucky enough to find an opening door or two,
he wasted little time pondering motives of pity or generosity;
for on that special night and perhaps for one night only,
our village wore a soft halo, almost akin to the *Little Town of
Bethlehem*'s.

Christmas Eve – Roseau

The throng rushes round on this last and most important shopping
   day,
eyes distracted.
Children clutch shopping bags bursting with presents to be wrapped.
Should I buy this, or this, or that?
Their parents smile indulgently.
From a shop window
a pink-faced, white-bearded Santa grins encouragement,
eyes crinkled in a conspiratorial wink.
The entire front is festooned in snow flakes
the temperature a mere eighty-five degrees.
I clutch a minutely folded ten dollar bill between damp fingers
and blink back unwelcome tears.
Empty handed, I retrace my steps, a tightness in my guts.

Meanwhile, back at my lodging house,
a large ham on the bone simmers on the stove;
hot loaves of crusty bread are cooling on the dresser
as too are rich, rum-soaked fruit cakes piping hot from the oven,
designed to melt upon the tongue.
Up on a shelf, a demijohn of day-old ginger beer gently settles;
bottles of sorrel spiced with cinnamon and cloves catch the light,
ruby red and pleasing to the eye,
much like the profusion of poinsettias in gardens everywhere
claiming their rightful place at the hearth of Christmastide.

Later, at midnight mass that night
my humble village church is replaced by an imposing cathedral,
all golden lights and candle holders gleaming.
Expensive dresses on display, rustle and swish
fit for a world-class fashion show,
while the choir from its rostrum effortlessly imitates a host of angels.
Hearts swell and beatific faces lift, perhaps in equal measure
to the gods of mammon as the God of heaven.

A bunch of urchins tease the drunk, lolling in a back pew.

He utters a string of profanities at which outraged grandees jerk in
    his direction,
a thousand eyes shooting daggers.
Meanwhile, the waifs, pictures of innocence,
heads bowed, kneel respectfully.

Up front, in a special little alcove lies the crib
where Baby Jesus, Mary and Joseph, sheep and shepherds look
    forlorn,
a touch incongruous,
rather like puzzled gate-crashers at their own party.

Christmas Eve – New York

It's Christmastime in the city
heaving sidewalks, frenzied shoppers
dazzling lights on Christmas trees
cash tills ringing
songs extolling sleigh bells, snow and Santa
Christ invisible, not there.

In the frenzied big day homage,
even midnight mass is rushed
and the church in Little Italy
on that cold and frosty night
stays devoid of joy or comfort
- no choir of angels here.

Call me Scrooge if you so choose
but Christmas Eve in that big city
belongs unequivocally to those
adept at peddling comfort and joy
to rainbow-chasers more than willing
if less able to pay for the privilege.

Christmas Eve – London

Too cold to venture out to midnight mass tonight
so I don't go
and anyway, carols from an ancient record player
just don't do the trick.
For a time, the excitement in the children's eyes
dancing in time to the flickering Christmas lights
is quite contagious,
as will be their enthusiasm and gratitude towards their modest gifts
of coloured pencils, water-colours and drawing pads.
One daughter has put up the tree while the other helped to bake the
    fruit cake,
its rich smells intoxicating from the kitchen.

For quite some time now, no joy from Christmas trees,
nor the pleasure of cake making,
for there's an empty chair
where the cake maker used to sit,
my gifts to her have most likely ended in the dust bin,
I have no way of knowing;
and so as not to wax unduly sad
over things as they now are,
I retire early on Christmas Eve
and pray for unbroken sleep till morning.

Haiku

it's raining again
what an inconvenience
when you're sleeping rough

the tears of rain-gods
blessed by those tucked up in bed
cursed by such as me

voices in their heads
persistent and controlling
such a life sentence

in my daughter's head
chickens dancing on our roof
for her ears only

hands outstretched towards
the most enormous chasm
waiting to be bridged

a cocktail of drugs
deep drowsiness inducer
sapping life away

carers' support group
talking, listening, sharing
we are not alone

from its estuary
soft White River titiwee
take themselves up stream

up at Belvedere
egrets feed on fattened ticks
hungry hawks hover